No nonsense Number Games

Ages 7–9   Book 3

Jackie Andrews • Jude Callaghan • Suzi de Gouveia

Title:	No Nonsense Number Games Ages 7-9 Book 3
Authors:	Suzi de Gouveia, Jackie Andrews and Jude Callaghan
Editor:	Tanya Tremewan
Designer:	Doreen Neason
Book code:	PB00143
ISBN:	978-1-908736-22-2
Published:	2012
Publisher:	TTS Group Ltd
	Park Lane Business Park Kirkby-in-Ashfield Notts, NG17 9GU Tel: 0800 318 686 Fax: 0800 137 525
Websites:	www.tts-shopping.com
Copyright:	Text: © Suzi de Gouveia, Jackie Andrews and Jude Callaghan, 2011 Edition and illustrations: © TTS Group Ltd, 2012
About the authors:	Suzi is the enthusiastic headteacher of St Teresa's Primary School in Christchurch, New Zealand who has international teaching experience. She has had the pleasure of teaching in a multi-cultural environment. Over 25 years of teaching have enabled Suzi to develop a wealth of ideas and resources to best help children.
	Jackie is an experienced teacher who has taught middle primary children in both New Zealand and the United Kingdom. As a mother of four young children she is beginning to wonder where the time to diversify has gone.
	Jude is an experienced, enthusiastic teacher with a passion for teaching and learning. Her teaching programmes are innovative and exciting. She has joined the writing team to share her deep understanding and wealth of ideas.

Copyright notice:

All right reserved. This book is sold subject to the condition that it shall not, by way of trade or otherwise, be lent, hired out or otherwise circulated without the publisher's prior consent in any form of binding or cover other than that in which it is published and with a similar condition, including this condition, being imposed upon the subsequent purchaser.

No part of this publication may be reproduced, stored in a retrieval system, or transmitted, in any form or by any means, electronic, mechanical, photocopying, recording or otherwise, without the prior permission of the publisher. This book remains copyright, although permission is granted to copy pages where indicated for classroom distribution and use only in the school which has purchased the book, or by the teacher who has purchased the book, and in accordance with the CLA licensing agreement. Photocopying permission is given only for purchasers and not for borrowers of books from any lending service.

Due to the nature of the web, the publisher cannot guarantee the content or links of any of the websites referred to. It is the responsibility of the reader to assess the suitability of websites.

Recognising multiplication facts

Overview: Abacus Times

Abacus Times has been designed to assist children to work out multiplication facts from existing knowledge.

Preparation and organisation

- Copy the abacus board (two per player) and the multiplication cards onto coloured paper.
- Laminate the boards and cards and cut out the cards.
- Store in a ziplock bag along with counters or a whiteboard pen.

I am learning to work out multiplication facts from ones I already know.

Abacus Times

Equipment needed

- Game cards
- Abacus boards
- Counters or whiteboard pen

Aim of the game

To show a multiplication problem on an abacus in two different ways (commutative property).

Playing instructions (one or two players)

- Each player has two abacus boards and the multiplication cards are face down in a pile.
- Each player takes a multiplication card from the pile.
- Each player shows the two ways of representing their multiplication problem on their two abacuses, using either counters or a whiteboard pen.

I am learning to recognise doubles and halves.

Double 'n' Halve Memory

Equipment needed
- Game cards

Aim of the game
To collect as many pairs of cards as possible, where each pair consists of either a number and its double or a number and its half.

Playing instructions (two players)
- Spread all of the cards face down over the floor or another large, flat surface.
- In turn each player turns over two cards.
- If the two cards consist of either a number and its double or a number and its half, the player sets them aside as a pair. If they do not match, the player puts them back in the same places face down.
- Play until all the cards have been paired up. The player who has collected more pairs is the winner.

1

I am learning to recognise doubles and halves.

Double 'n' Halve Snap

Equipment needed
- Game cards

Aim of the game
To get all of the game cards.

Playing instructions (two players)
- Deal out all the cards equally between the players, who hold their own cards face down in a small pile.
- In turn, each player places their top card face up in the middle.
- If the card they place is either double or half of the card that is immediately underneath it in the middle pile, both of the players race to be first to "snap" the pile. The player who is first gets the pile and puts it at the bottom of their own pile of cards.
- The game continues until one player has all the cards.

1

Recognising doubles and halves

Overview: Double 'n' Halve Beans, Memory and Snap

Double 'n' Halve Beans, Memory and Snap are three games designed to assist children to recognise doubles and halves of numbers.

Preparation and organisation

- Copy the game cards onto coloured paper.
- Laminate and cut out the cards.
- Store in a ziplock bag. For Double 'n' Halve Beans, include four small bean bags as well.

I am learning to recognise doubles and halves.

Double 'n' Halve Beans

Equipment needed

- Two bean bags
- Game cards
- Pen and paper for record keeping

Aim of the game

To collect two pairs of game cards, where each pair consists of either a number and its double or a number and its half.

Playing instructions (three players)

- The dealer shuffles all the cards, deals out four to each player and places the remaining cards face down in a pile by their side.
- The dealer picks up the top card from this pile, assesses their cards and passes one unwanted card to the second player. This second player then assesses their cards and passes one unwanted card to the third player.
- The third player puts their own unwanted card into a discard pile.
- When a player has two pairs, they grab a bean bag. The other two players race to take the remaining bean bag.
- The player with the two pairs shows them for the other players to verify. If both pairs are correct, the player without a bean bag gets one letter towards the spelling of *beans*.
- Rounds continue in this way. The first player to spell *beans* is out.

Introduction

This set of games books in the *No Nonsense Number* series has been designed to help busy teachers provide children in their class with activities that contribute to the achievement of an identified learning objectives. Games are an enjoyable way of reinforcing learning. They can also be sent home for the children to play with their families, providing more repetition for the children as well as involving families and showing them what their children are learning.

Each game comes with an instruction card that includes the learning objective. Any related content cards required for the game are also provided here and just need to be photocopied. We suggest that, to assist with classroom organisation, you copy the cards for each level in one specific colour. The instruction cards and game cards all have a code on them to help sort out mixed-up cards.

Another useful arrangement each time a group plays a game is for the group to begin with a pile of 10 counters set aside. Each time someone wins a game, that child takes one counter. This system will show who the overall winner is and ensures that each game is played 10 times.

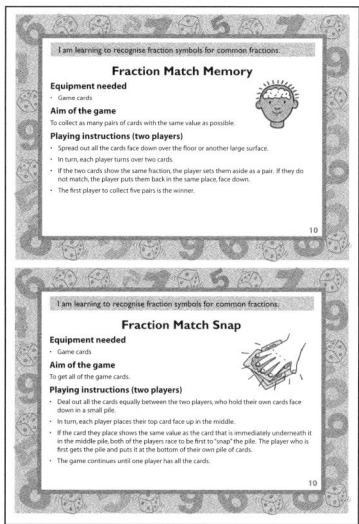

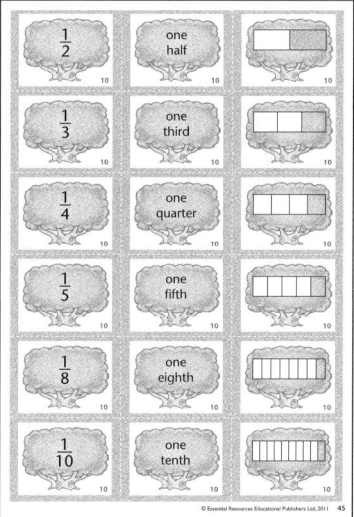

Contents

Introduction	4
Recognising doubles and halves	**5**
Double 'n' Halve Beans	5
Double 'n' Halve Memory	6
Double 'n' Halve Snap	6
Recognising multiplication facts	**11**
Abacus Times	11
Recalling number facts	**15**
Spider Foot Facts	15
Recalling groupings within 10 and 100	**17**
Making 10 Snap	17
Making 100 Snap	19
Recalling addition and multiplication facts	**23**
Bigger or Smaller?	23
Multiplication Bingo	30
Recognising the numbers before and after	**34**
Build Your Maths Muscles	34
Applying place value knowledge	**36**
Place Value Train Beans	36
Place Value Train Snap	37
Place Value Train Memory	37
Recognising fractions	**43**
Fraction Match Beans	43
Fraction Match Memory	44
Fraction Match Snap	44
Recognising mixed numbers	**51**
Fraction Rummy	51
Fraction Memory	52
Fraction Snap	52

Recalling number facts

Overview: Spider Foot Facts

Spider Foot Facts has been designed to reinforce number facts.

Preparation and organisation

- Make multiple copies of the spider board onto coloured paper.
- On each board, write the first number of the four equations in the four feet on the left-hand side, and the operation and the second number on the body.
- Laminate the boards.
- Store in a ziplock bag along with a whiteboard pen.

I am learning to recall number facts.

Spider Foot Facts

Equipment needed

- Spider boards
- Whiteboard pen

Aim of the game

To complete the basic facts and fill in the empty spider feet.

Playing instructions (one player)

- Choose a spider board and complete the equation by writing the four answers in the spider's feet.
- Swap your board with a friend's and check each other's answers.

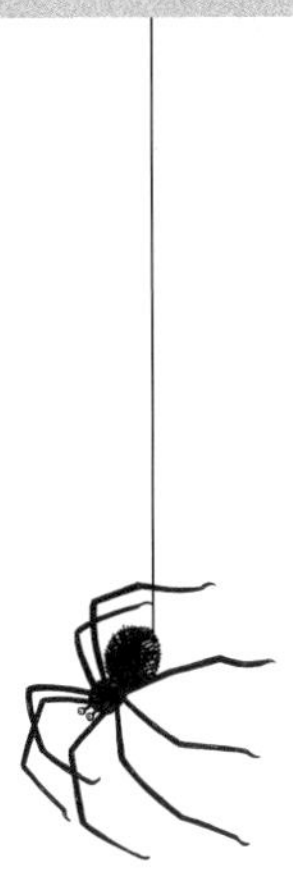

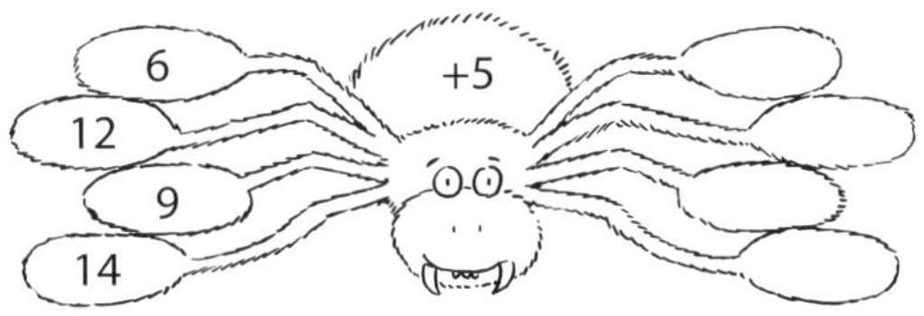

6   +5
12
 9
14

3

3

Recalling groupings within 10

Overview: Making 10 Snap

Making 10 Snap has been designed to help children identify pairs of numbers that make 10 when added together.

Preparation and organisation

- Make two copies of the page of game cards on coloured paper.
- Laminate and cut out the cards.
- Store in a ziplock bag.

I am learning to recognise numbers that make 10.

Making 10 Snap

Equipment needed

- Game cards

Aim of the game

To get all of the game cards.

Playing instructions (two players)

- Deal out all the cards equally between the players, who hold their own cards face down in a small pile.
- In turn, each player places their top card face up in the middle.
- If the card they place and the card that is immediately underneath it in the middle pile add up to 10, both of the players race to be first to "snap" the pile. The player who is first gets the pile and puts it at the bottom of their own pile of cards.
- The game continues until one player has all the cards.

Recalling groupings within 100

Overview: Making 100 Snap

Making 100 Snap has been designed to help children identify pairs of numbers that make 100 when added together.

Preparation and organisation

- Make two copies of each page of game cards on coloured paper.
- Laminate and cut out the cards.
- Store in a ziplock bag.

I am learning to recognise numbers that make 100.

Making 100 Snap

Equipment needed
- Game cards

Aim of the game
To get all of the game cards.

Playing instructions (two players)

- Deal out all the cards equally between the players, who hold their own cards face down in a small pile.
- In turn, each player places their top card face up in the middle.
- If the card they place makes 100 when added to the card that is immediately underneath it in the middle pile, both of the players race to be first to "snap" the pile. The player who is first gets the pile and puts it at the bottom of their own pile of cards.
- The game continues until one player has all the cards.

5

© TTS Group Ltd, 2012

Recalling addition and multiplication facts

Overview: Bigger or Smaller?

Bigger or Smaller? has been designed to reinforce the recall of addition and multiplication facts.

Preparation and organisation

- Copy each set of game cards (multiplication and addition) onto a different coloured paper.
- Copy one set of three symbol cards for each player.
- Laminate and cut the cards.
- Store in a ziplock bag.

I am learning to recall addition and multiplication facts.

Bigger or Smaller?

Equipment needed

- Game cards
- Symbol cards (one set per player)

Aim of the game

To be the first to use the correct symbol to compare the value of the two problems.

Playing instructions (two players)

- Choose a set of game cards and deal them out equally between the two players.
- Each player places their game cards in a pile face down, and has their three symbol cards face up in front of them.
- Starting at the same time each player turns over the top game card in their pile and puts it in the middle.
- Each player tries to be first to place the correct symbol card between the two game cards to make the statement true. The one who is first gets to keep the game cards.
- The game continues until all the game cards have been used. The player with more cards is the winner.

6

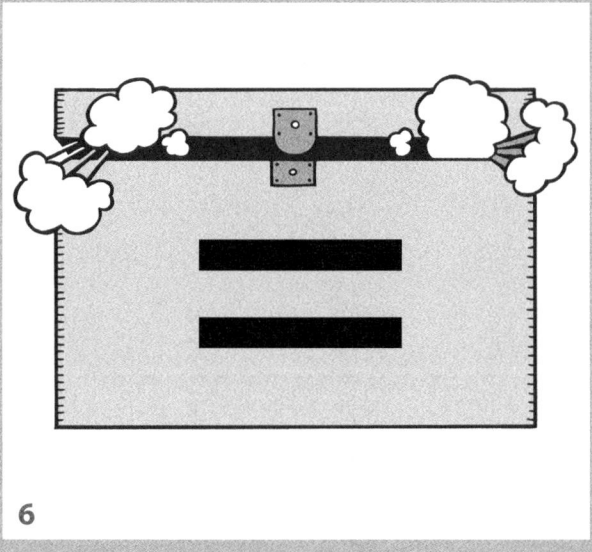
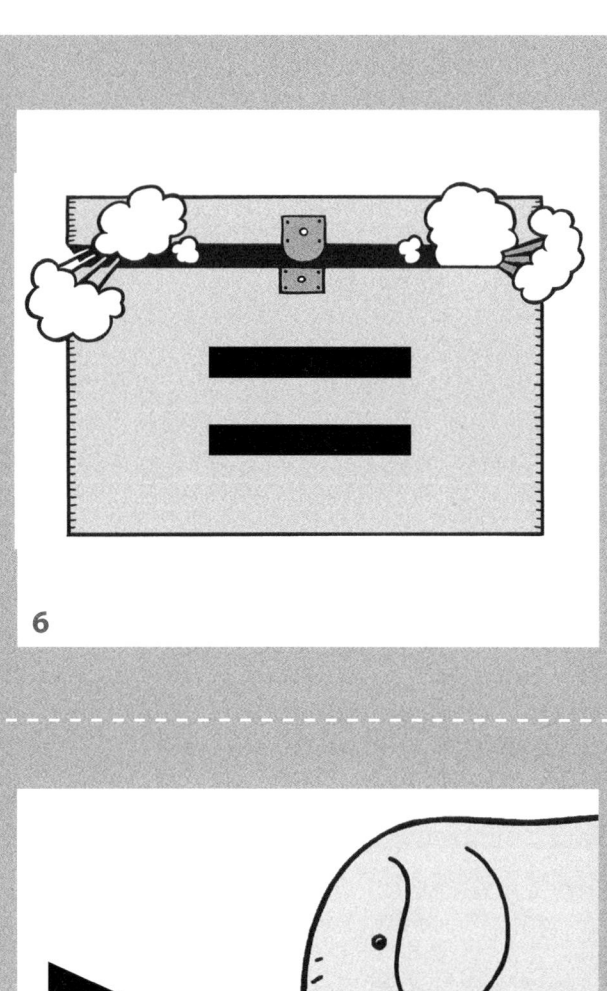

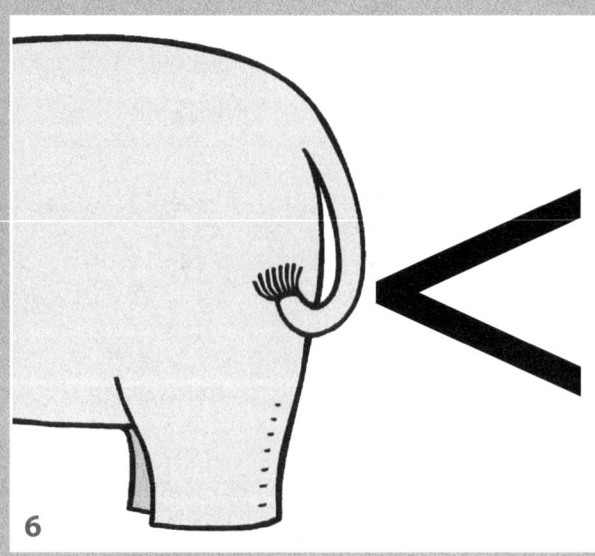

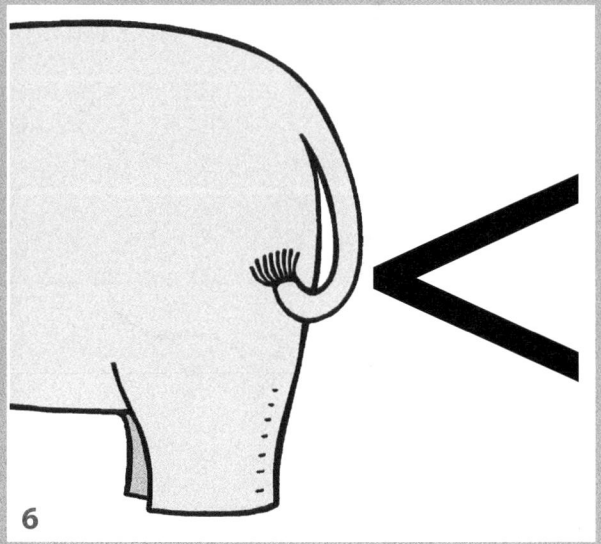

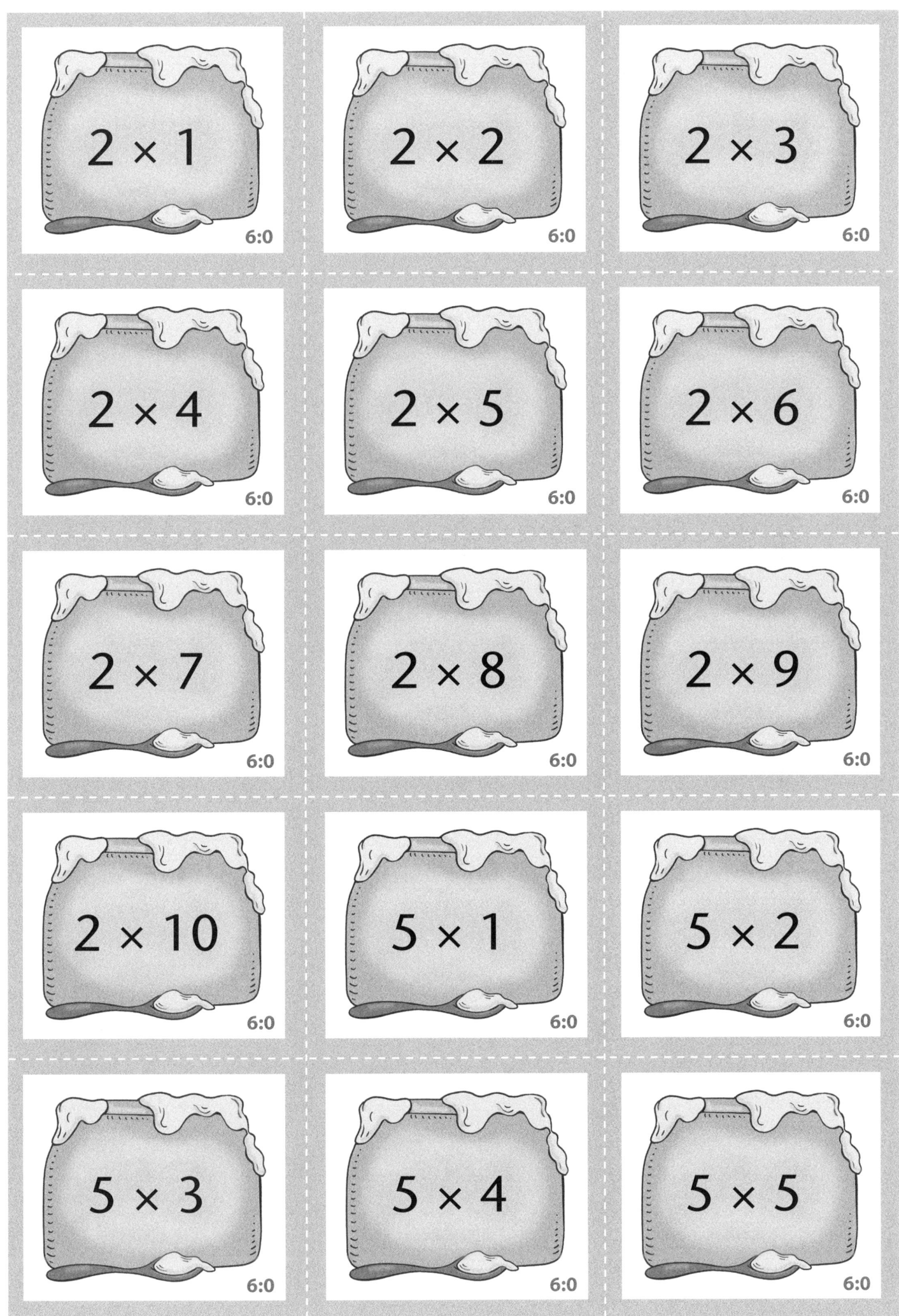

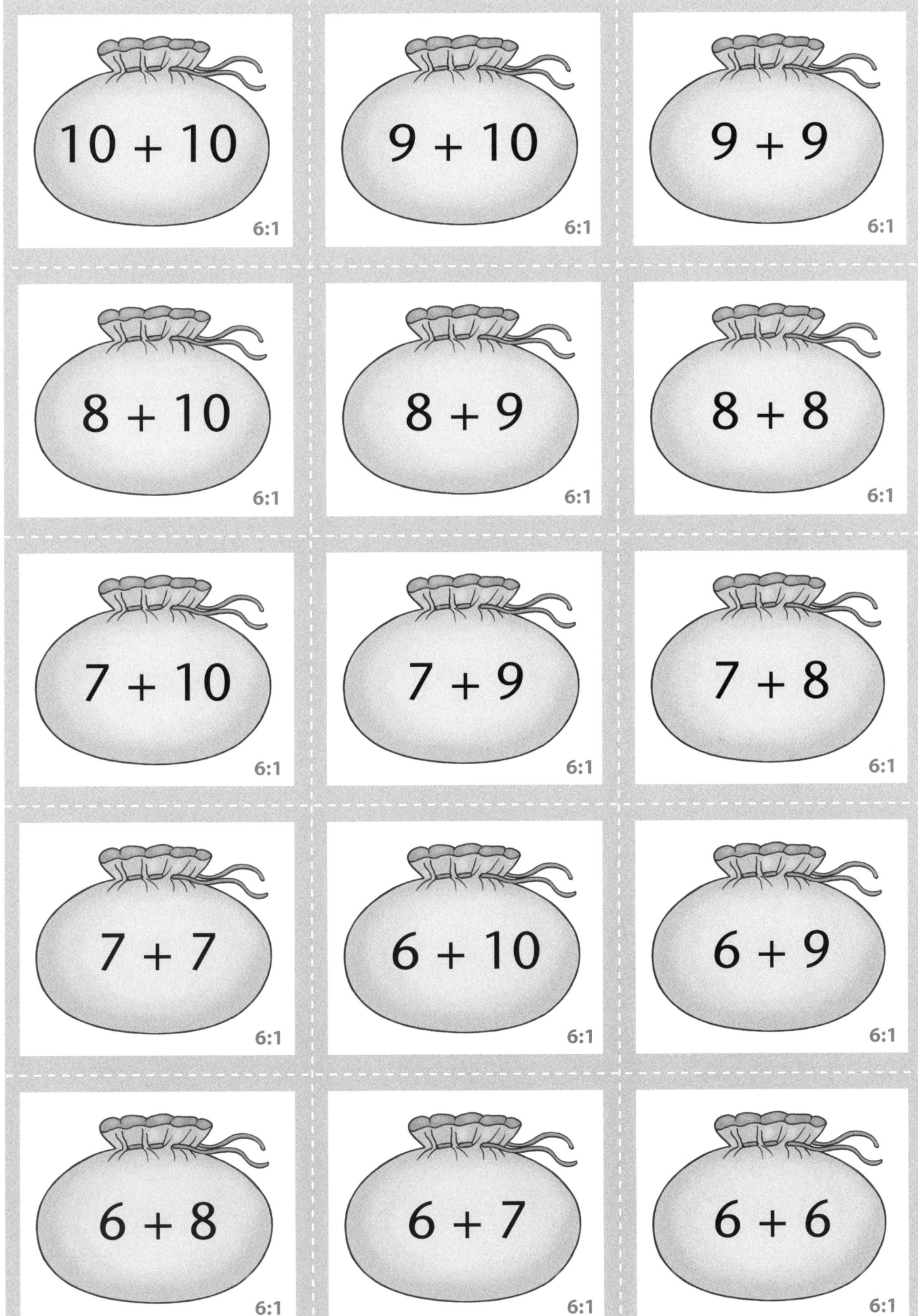

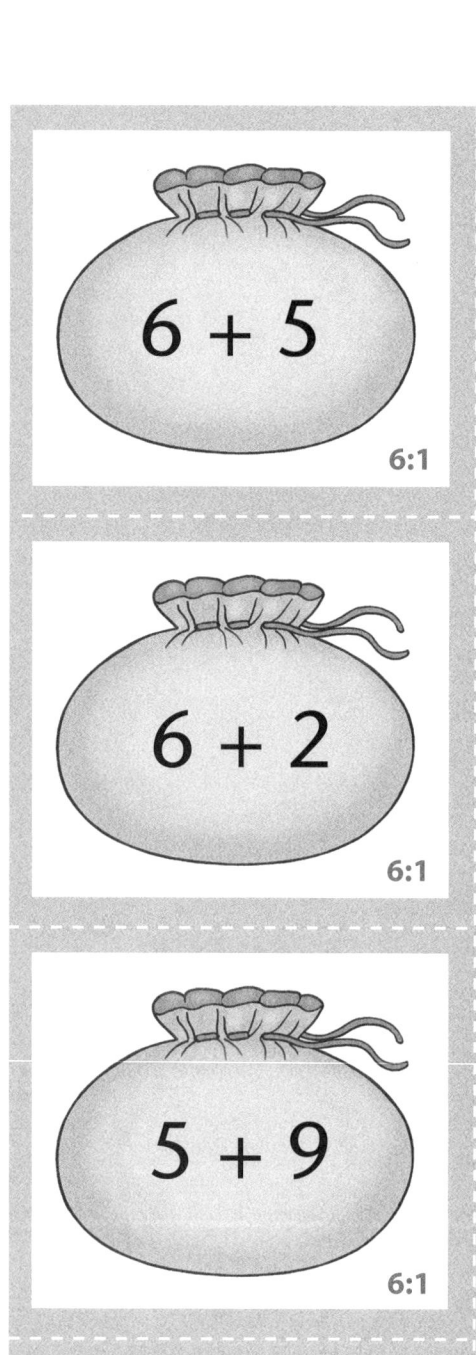
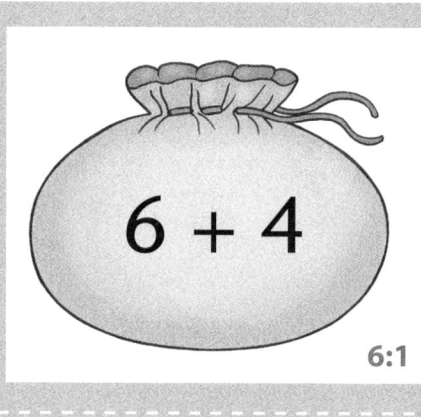
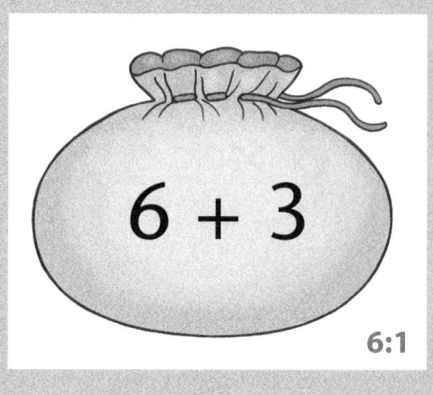
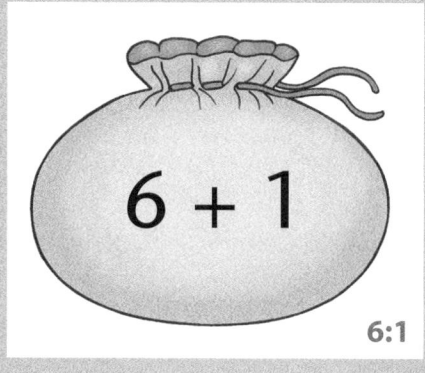

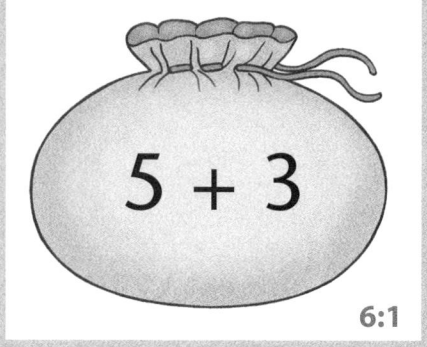

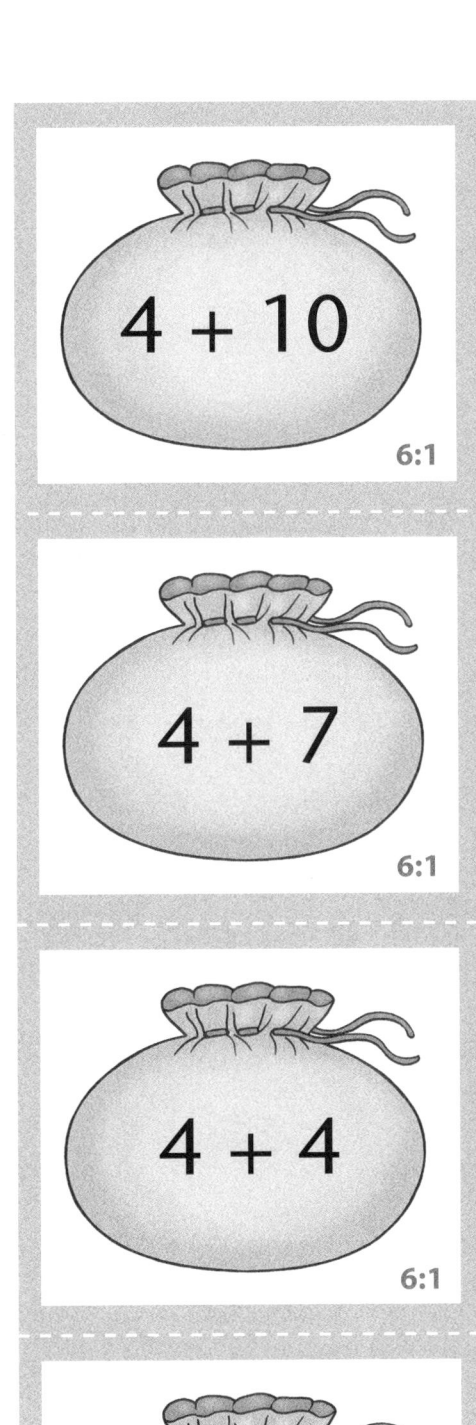
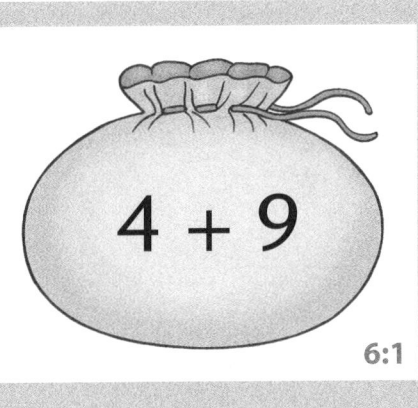

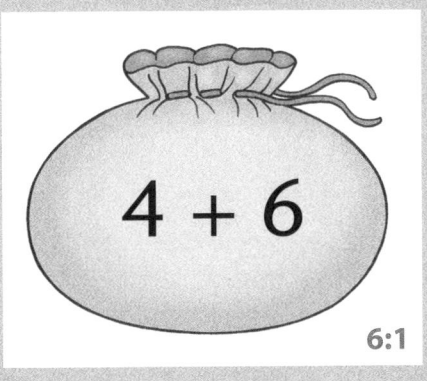
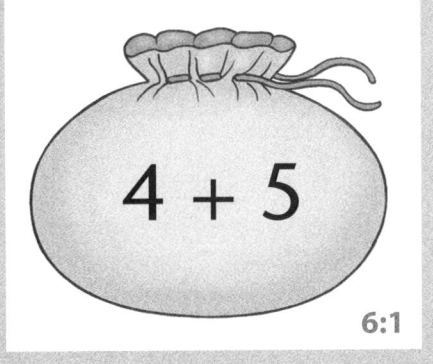
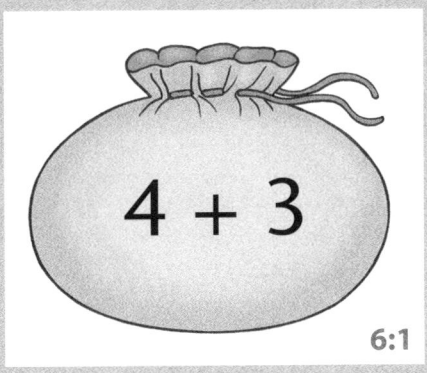

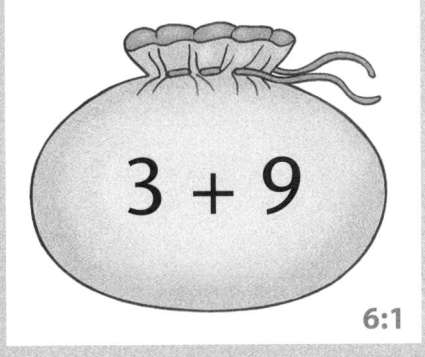

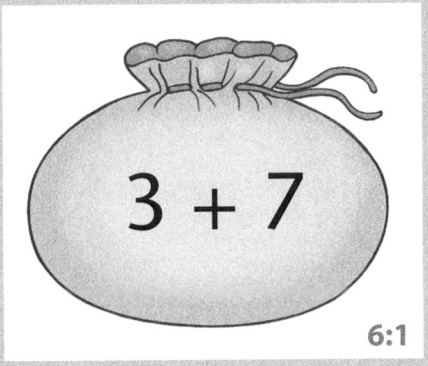

Recalling multiplication facts

Overview: Multiplication Bingo

Multiplication Bingo is designed to reinforce the children's recall of multiplication facts.

Preparation and organisation

- Copy the bingo boards onto coloured paper, then laminate and cut them out and store in a ziplock bag along with counters for covering numbers.
- Copy, laminate and cut out a set of calling cards and store them in a ziplock bag.

I am learning to recall my multiplication facts.

Multiplication Bingo

Equipment needed

- Bingo boards
- Calling cards
- Counters

Aim of the game

To be the first to complete a bingo board.

Playing instructions (up to four players)

- Nominate one player to be the caller.
- Each other player has one or more bingo boards.
- The caller reads out one calling card (containing a multiplication problem) at a time.
- If any player has the answer to that problem on their bingo board, they cover it on their board with a counter.
- The first player to cover all the numbers on their card calls out, "Bingo".

7

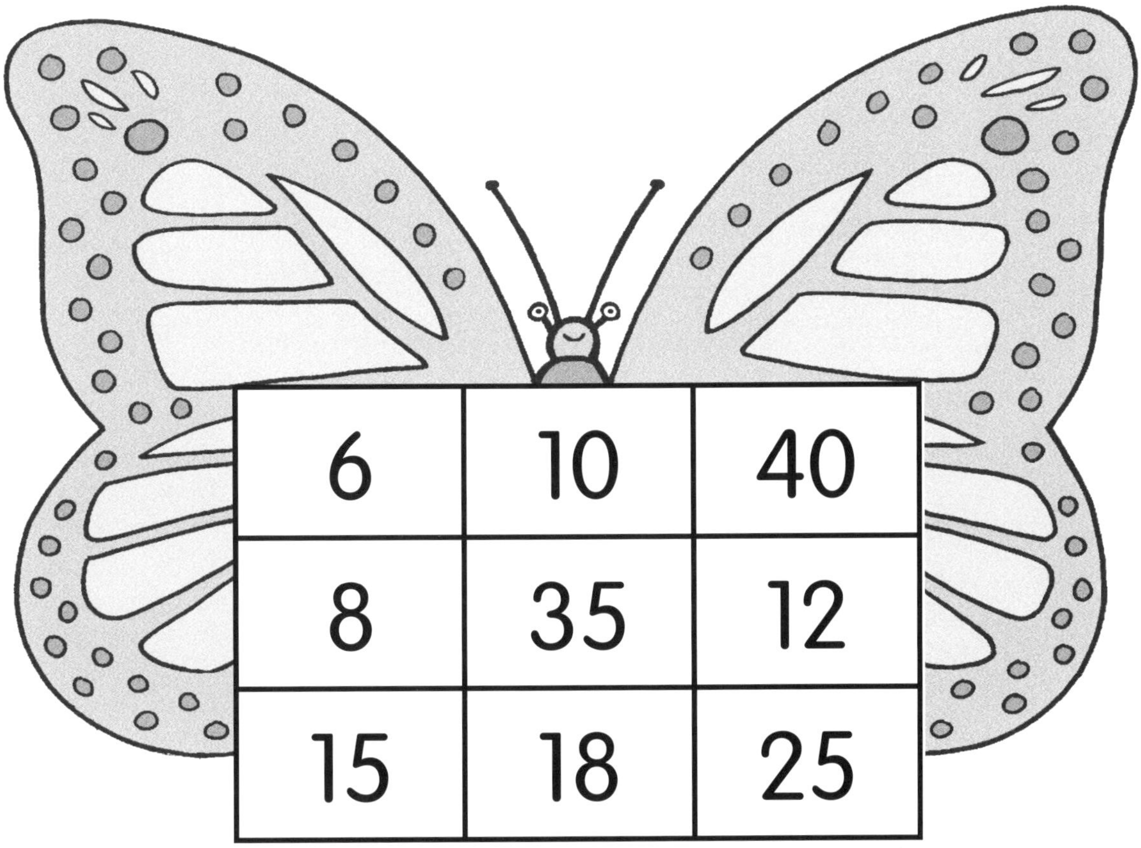

6	10	40
8	35	12
15	18	25

7

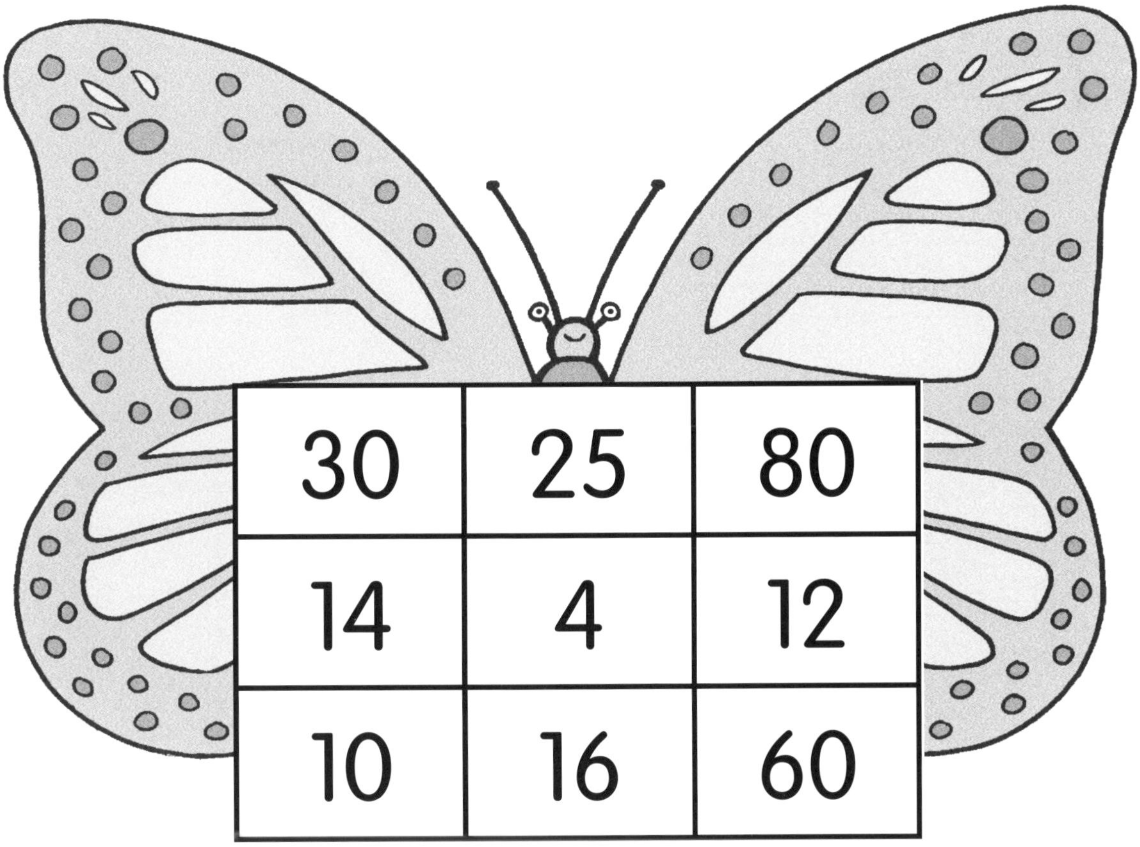

30	25	80
14	4	12
10	16	60

7

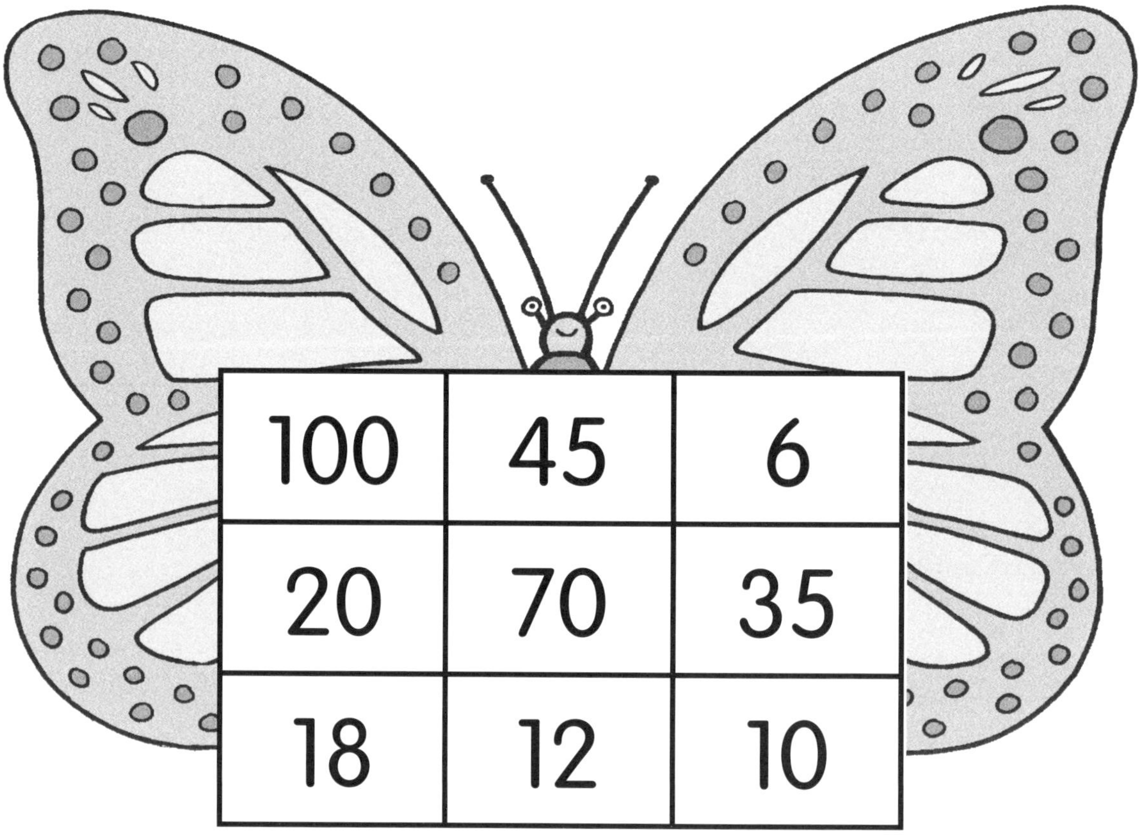

100	45	6
20	70	35
18	12	10

7

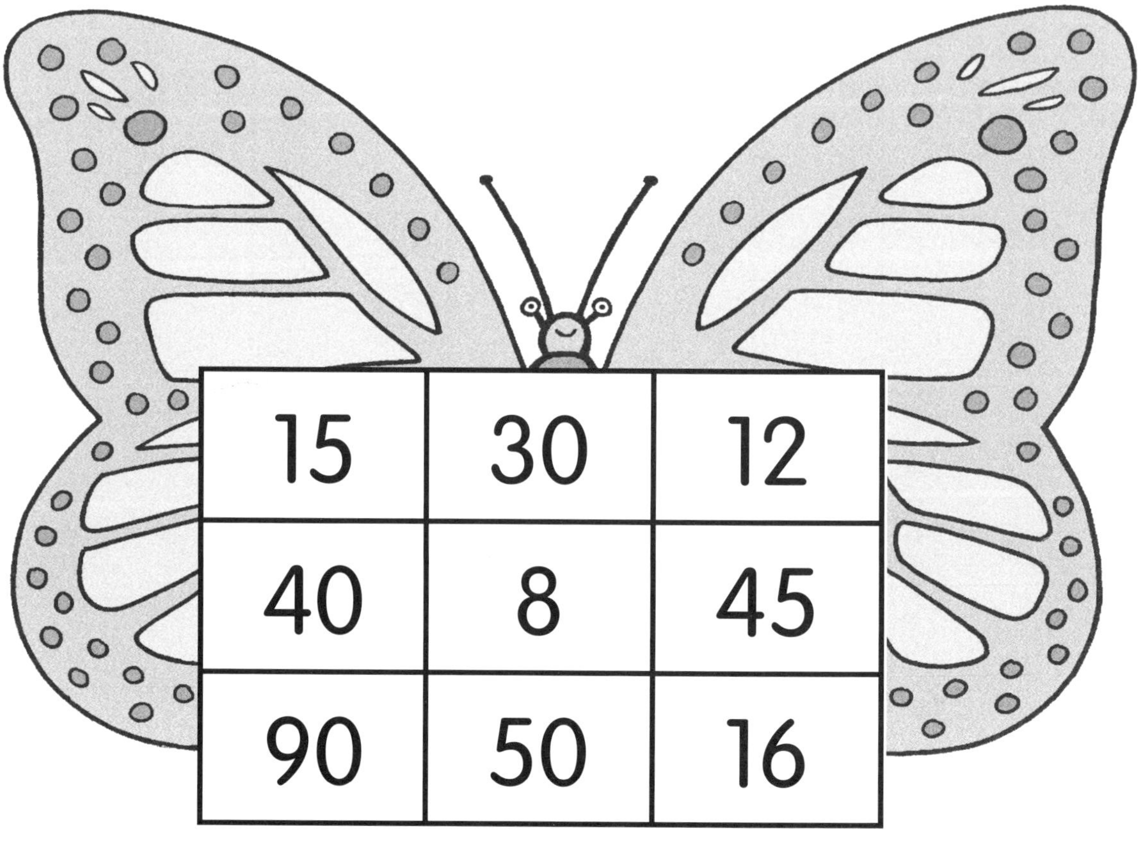

15	30	12
40	8	45
90	50	16

7

2 × 2	5 × 2	10 × 2
2 × 3	5 × 3	10 × 3
2 × 4	5 × 4	10 × 4
2 × 5	5 × 5	10 × 5
2 × 6	5 × 6	10 × 6
2 × 7	5 × 7	10 × 7
2 × 8	5 × 8	10 × 8
2 × 9	5 × 9	10 × 9
2 × 10	5 × 10	10 × 10

Recognising the numbers before and after

Overview: Build Your Maths Muscles

Build Your Maths Muscles comprises practice sheets designed to help children reinforce their recognition of the numbers 10, 100 and 1 000 more and 10 and 100 less.

Preparation and organisation

- Make multiple copies of the practice sheet onto coloured paper.
- Fill in three-digit numbers in the left-hand column.
- Laminate the practice sheets with the left-hand column completed.
- Store in a ziplock bag along with a whiteboard pen.

I am learning to recognise the number before and the number after.

Build Your Maths Muscles

Equipment needed
- Practice sheets
- Whiteboard pen

Aim of the game

To fill in all the missing numbers on the practice sheet.

Playing instructions (one player)
- Fill in the missing numbers on the practice sheet.
- Swap your completed sheet with a friend for them to check.

8

10 more	10 less	100 more	100 less	1 000 more

Applying place value knowledge

Overview: Place Value Train Beans, Snap and Memory

Place Value Train Beans, Snap and Memory are three games designed to help children apply their place value knowledge.

Preparation and organisation

- Copy the engine cards and carriage cards onto coloured paper.
- Laminate and cut out the cards.
- Store in a ziplock bag. For Place Value Train Beans, include four small bean bags as well.

I am learning to apply my place value knowledge.

Place Value Train Beans

Equipment needed

- Two bean bags
- Engine cards
- Carriage cards
- Pen and paper for record keeping

Aim of the game

To collect one engine card and three carriage cards that all have the same value.

Playing instructions (three players)

- The dealer shuffles all the cards, deals out four to each player and places the remaining cards face down in a pile by their side.
- The dealer picks up the top card from this pile, assesses their cards and passes one unwanted card to the second player. This second player then assesses their cards and passes one unwanted card to the third player.
- The third player puts their own unwanted card into a discard pile.
- When a player has one engine card matched with three carriage cards, they grab a bean bag. The other two players race to take the remaining bean bag.
- The player with the completed train shows it for the other players to verify. If it is correct, the player without a bean bag gets one letter towards the spelling of *beans*.
- Rounds continue in this way. The first person to spell *beans* is out.

9

I am learning to apply my place value knowledge.

Place Value Train Snap

Equipment needed
- Engine cards
- Carriage cards

Aim of the game
To get all of the cards.

Playing instructions (two players)
- Deal out all the cards equally between the players who hold their own cards face down in a small pile.
- In turn, each player places the top card in their pile face up in the middle.
- If the card they place has the same value as the card that is immediately underneath it in the middle pile, both of the children race to be first to "snap" the pile. The player who is first gets the pile and puts it at the bottom of their own pile of cards.
- The game continues until one player has all the cards.

9

I am learning to apply my place value knowledge.

Place Value Train Memory

Equipment needed
- Engine cards
- Carriage cards

Aim of the game
To make as many four-carriage trains as possible.

Playing instructions (two players)
- Spread all of the carriage cards face down over the floor or another large, flat surface.
- Deal the engine cards out equally between the two players, who are allowed to look at their share of engine cards.
- In turn, each player turns over one carriage card.
- If the carriage card has the same value as one of their engine cards, the player adds it to the engine. When they have collected four carriages with the same value, they have a complete train and set it aside.
- Play until all the cards have been matched up. The player who has collected the higher number of complete trains is the winner.

9

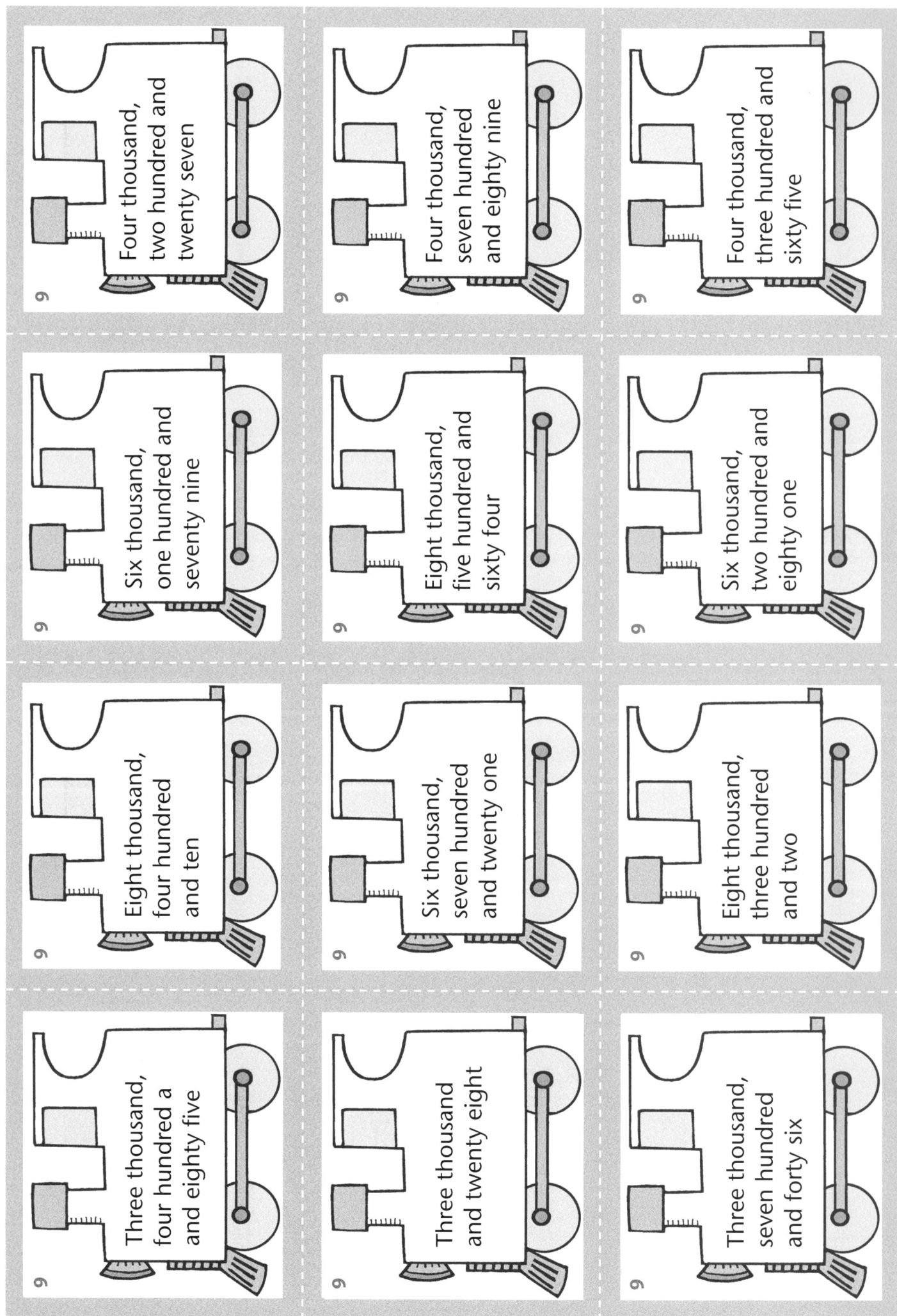

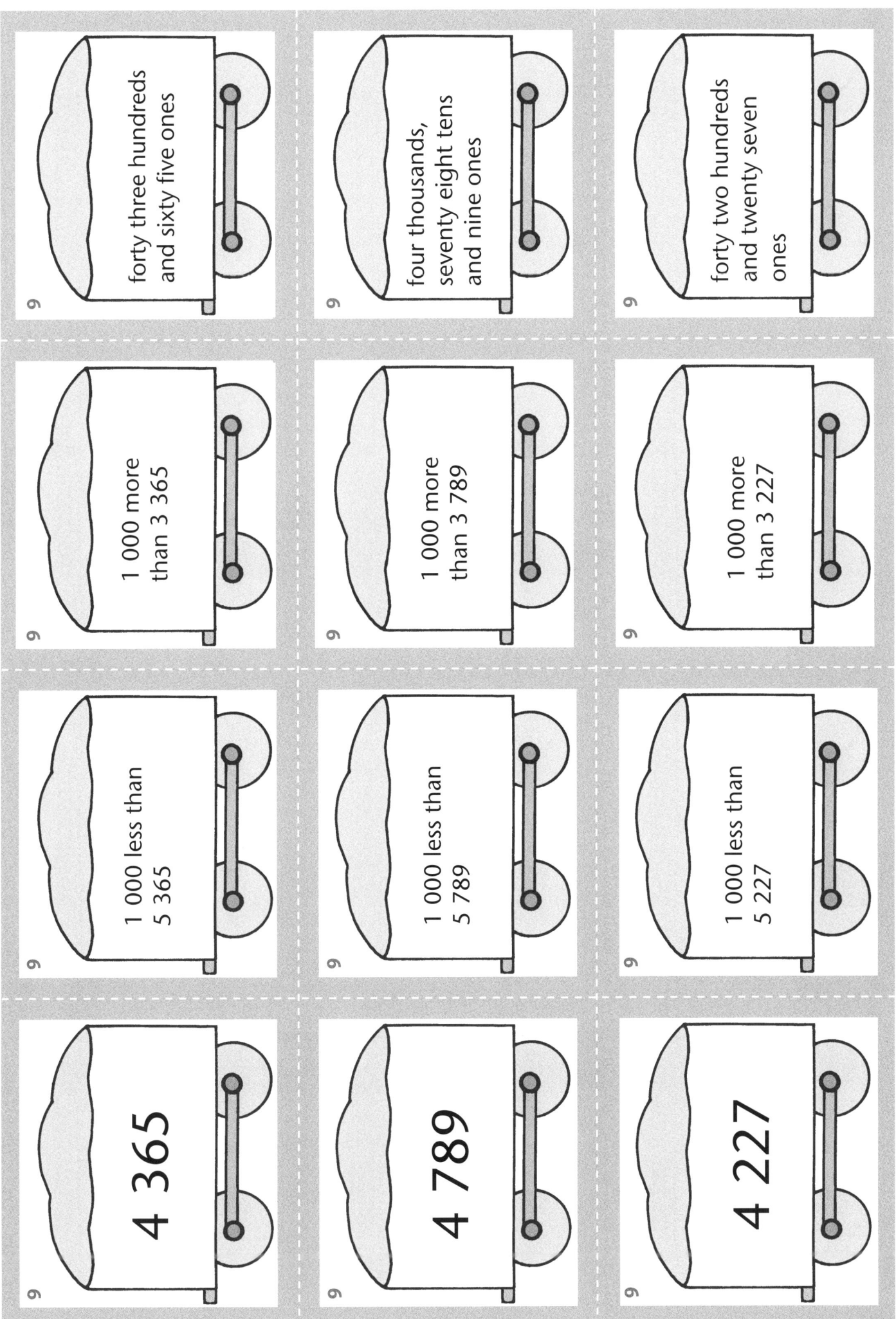

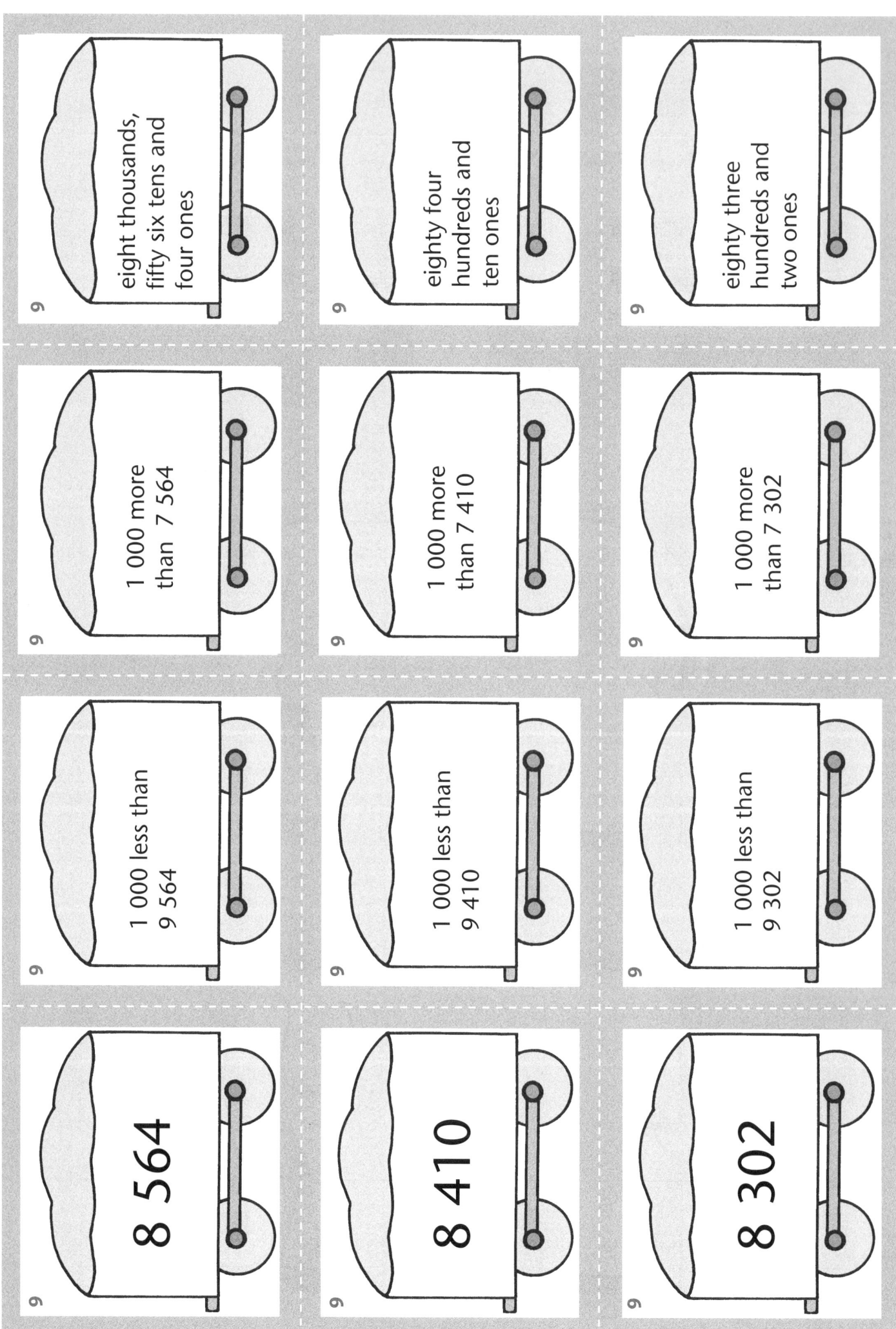

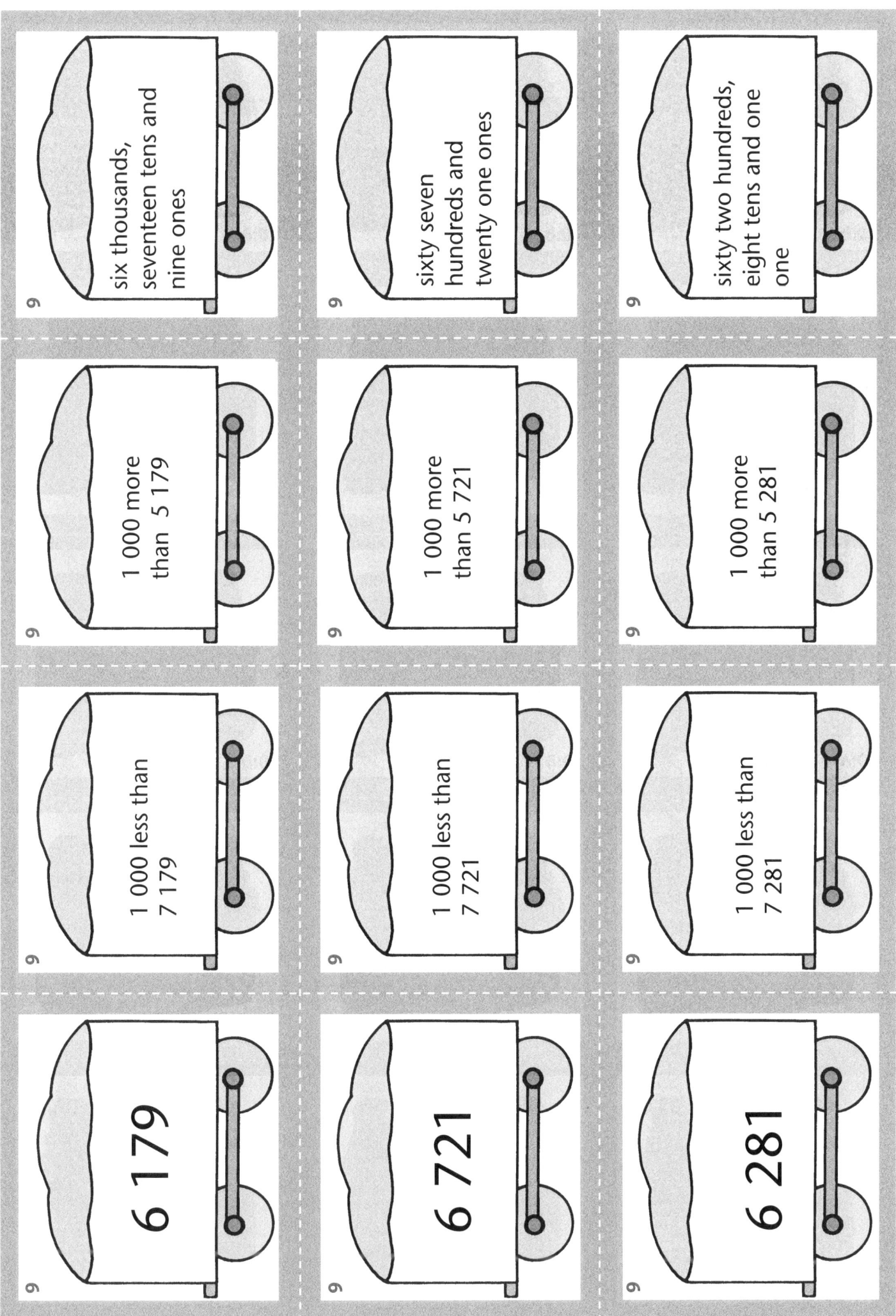

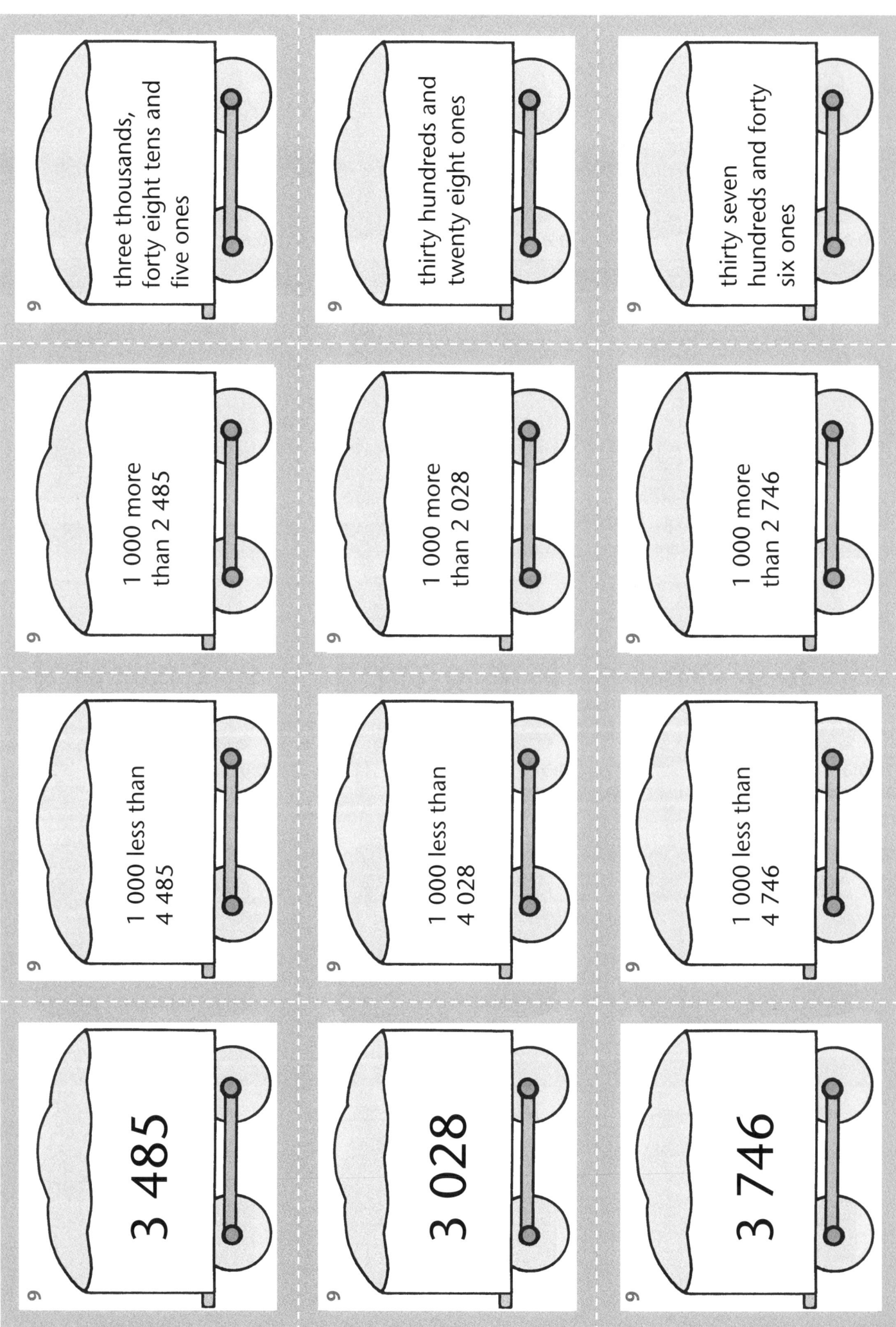

Recognising fractions

Overview: Fraction Match Beans, Memory and Snap

Fraction Match Beans, Memory and Snap are three games designed to help children recognise fraction symbols for common fractions.

Preparation and organisation

- Copy a set of game cards onto coloured paper.
- Laminate and cut out the cards.
- Store in a ziplock bag. For Fraction Match Beans, include four small bean bags as well.

I am learning to recognise fraction symbols for common fractions.

Fraction Match Beans

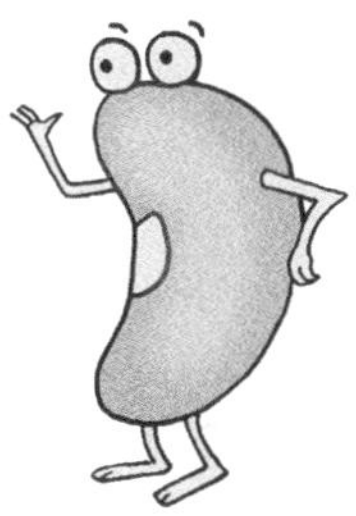

Equipment needed

- Two bean bags
- Game cards
- Pen and paper for record keeping

Aim of the game

To collect three game cards that all have the same value.

Playing instructions (three players)

- The dealer shuffles all the cards, deals out four to each player and places the remaining cards face down in a pile by their side.
- The dealer picks up the top card from this pile, assesses their cards and passes one unwanted card to the second player. This second player then assesses their cards and passes one unwanted card to the third player.
- The third player puts their own unwanted card into a discard pile.
- When a player has three matching cards, they grab a bean bag. The other two players race to take the remaining bean bag.
- The player with the three matching cards shows them for the other players to verify. If they are correct, the player without a bean bag gets one letter towards the spelling of *beans*.
- Rounds continue in this way. The first person to spell *beans* is out.

10

© TTS Group Ltd, 2012

I am learning to recognise fraction symbols for common fractions.

Fraction Match Memory

Equipment needed
- Game cards

Aim of the game

To collect as many pairs of cards with the same value as possible.

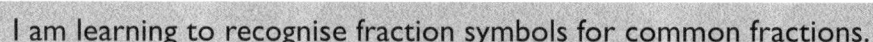

Playing instructions (two players)
- Spread out all the cards face down over the floor or another large surface.
- In turn, each player turns over two cards.
- If the two cards show the same fraction, the player sets them aside as a pair. If they do not match, the player puts them back in the same place, face down.
- The first player to collect five pairs is the winner.

10

I am learning to recognise fraction symbols for common fractions.

Fraction Match Snap

Equipment needed
- Game cards

Aim of the game

To get all of the game cards.

Playing instructions (two players)
- Deal out all the cards equally between the two players, who hold their own cards face down in a small pile.
- In turn, each player places their top card face up in the middle.
- If the card they place shows the same value as the card that is immediately underneath it in the middle pile, both of the players race to be first to "snap" the pile. The player who is first gets the pile and puts it at the bottom of their own pile of cards.
- The game continues until one player has all the cards.

10

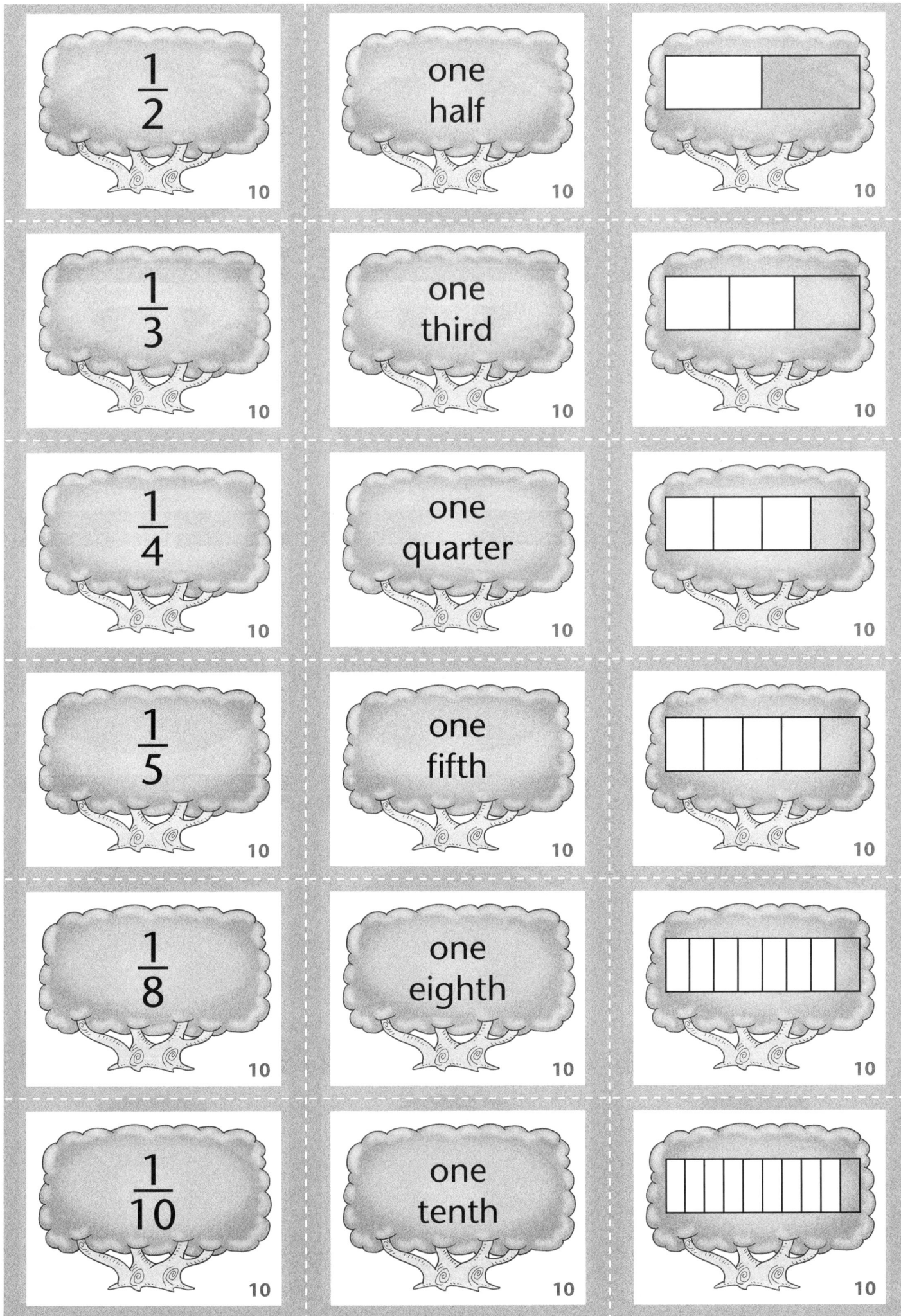

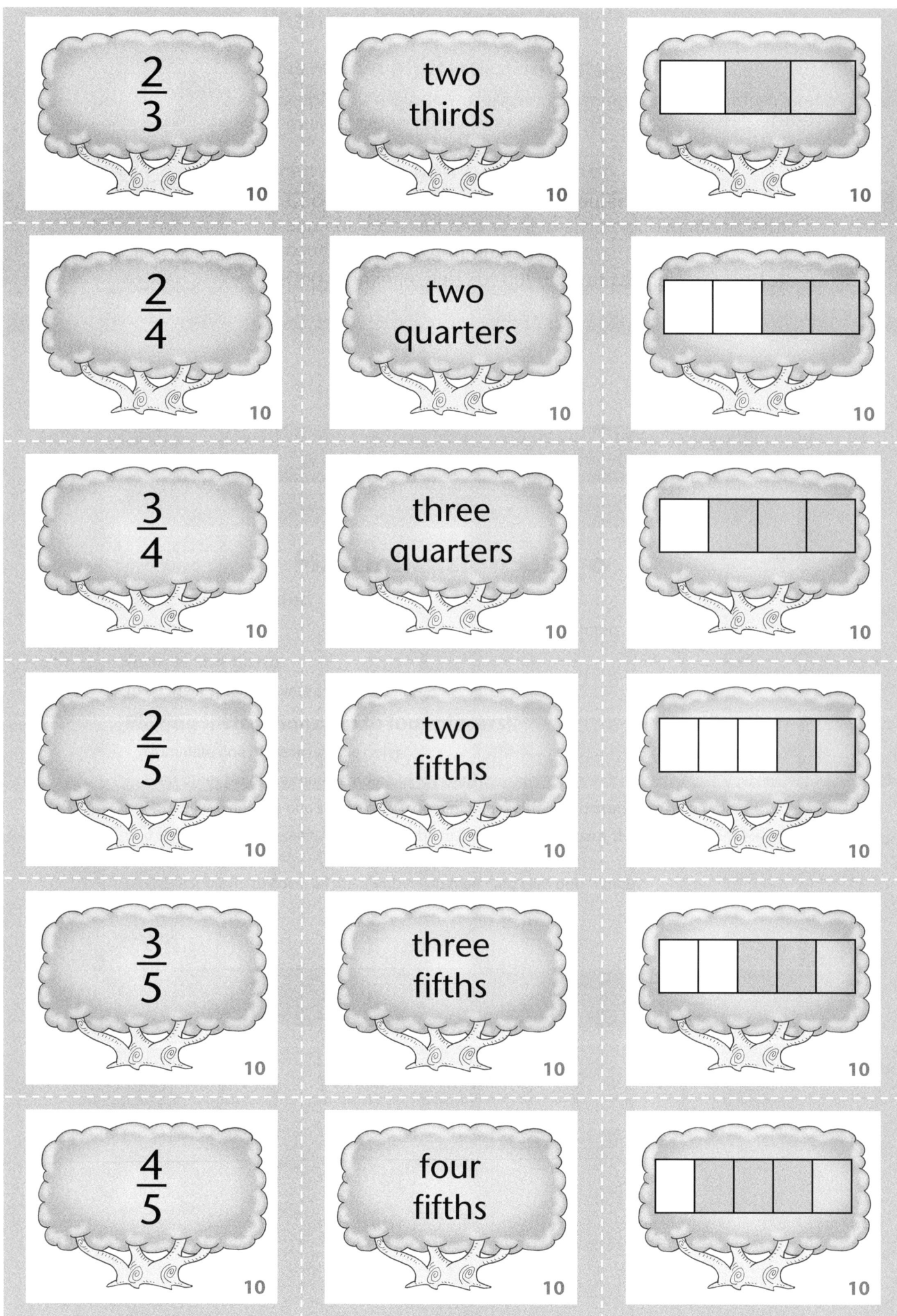

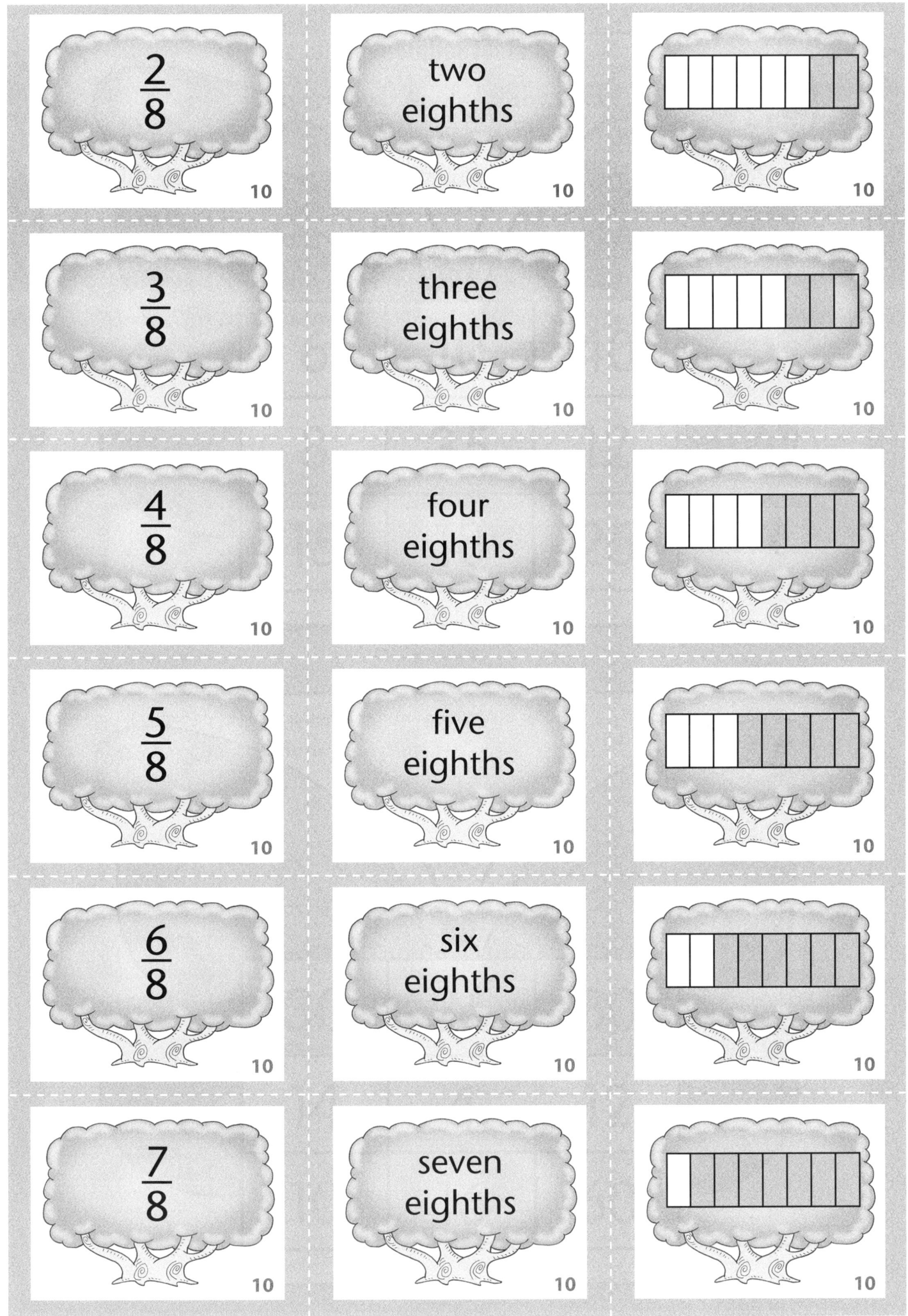

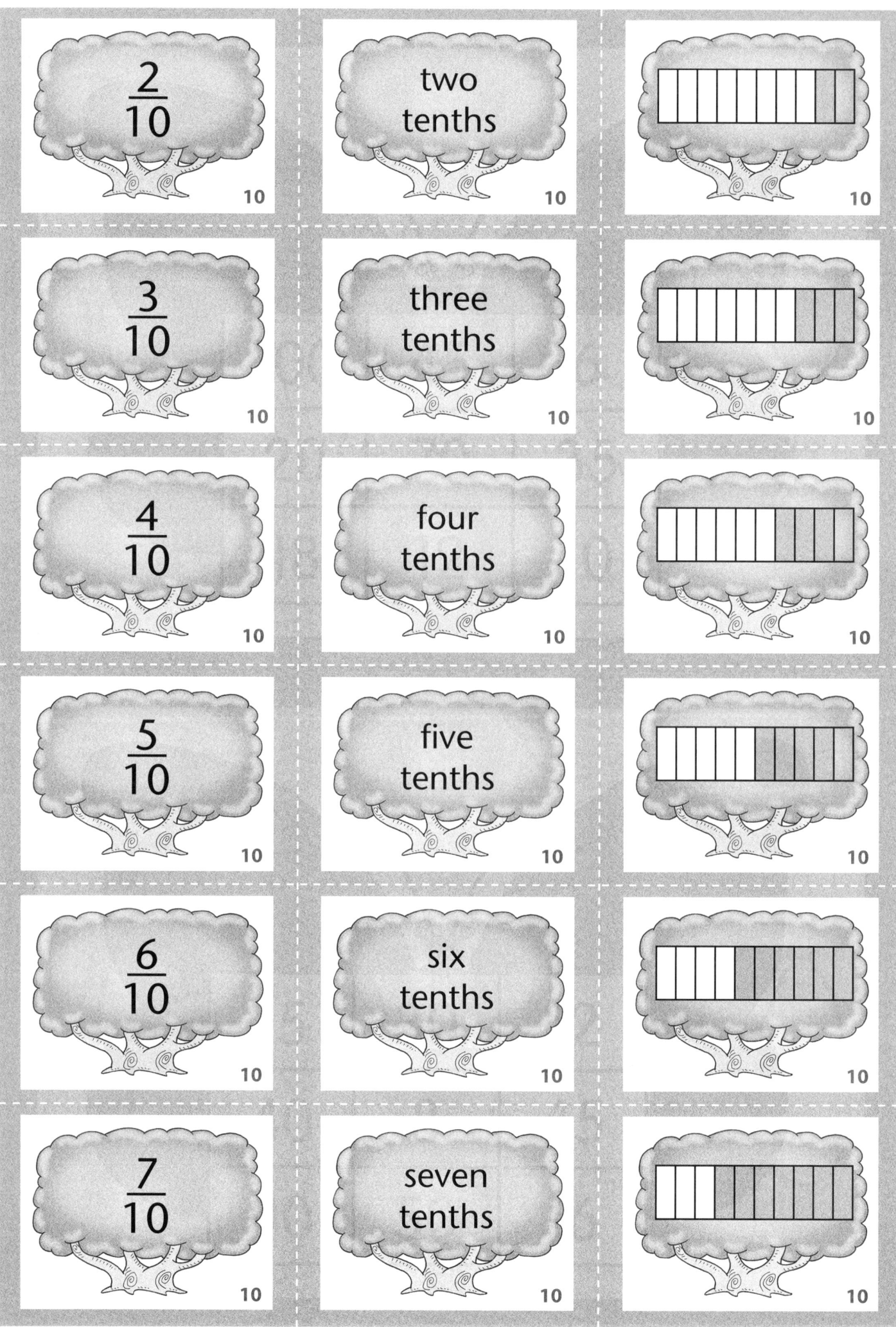

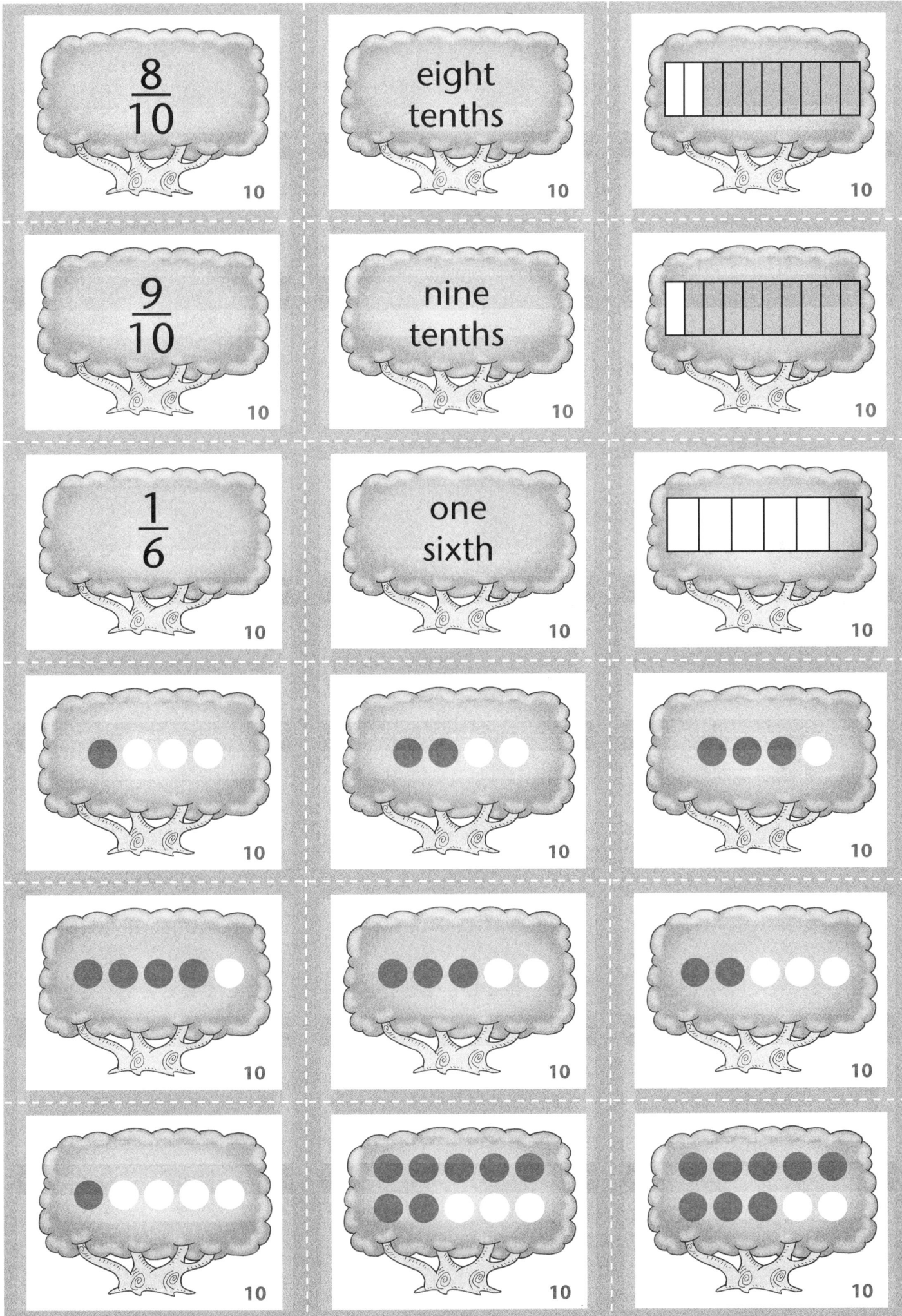

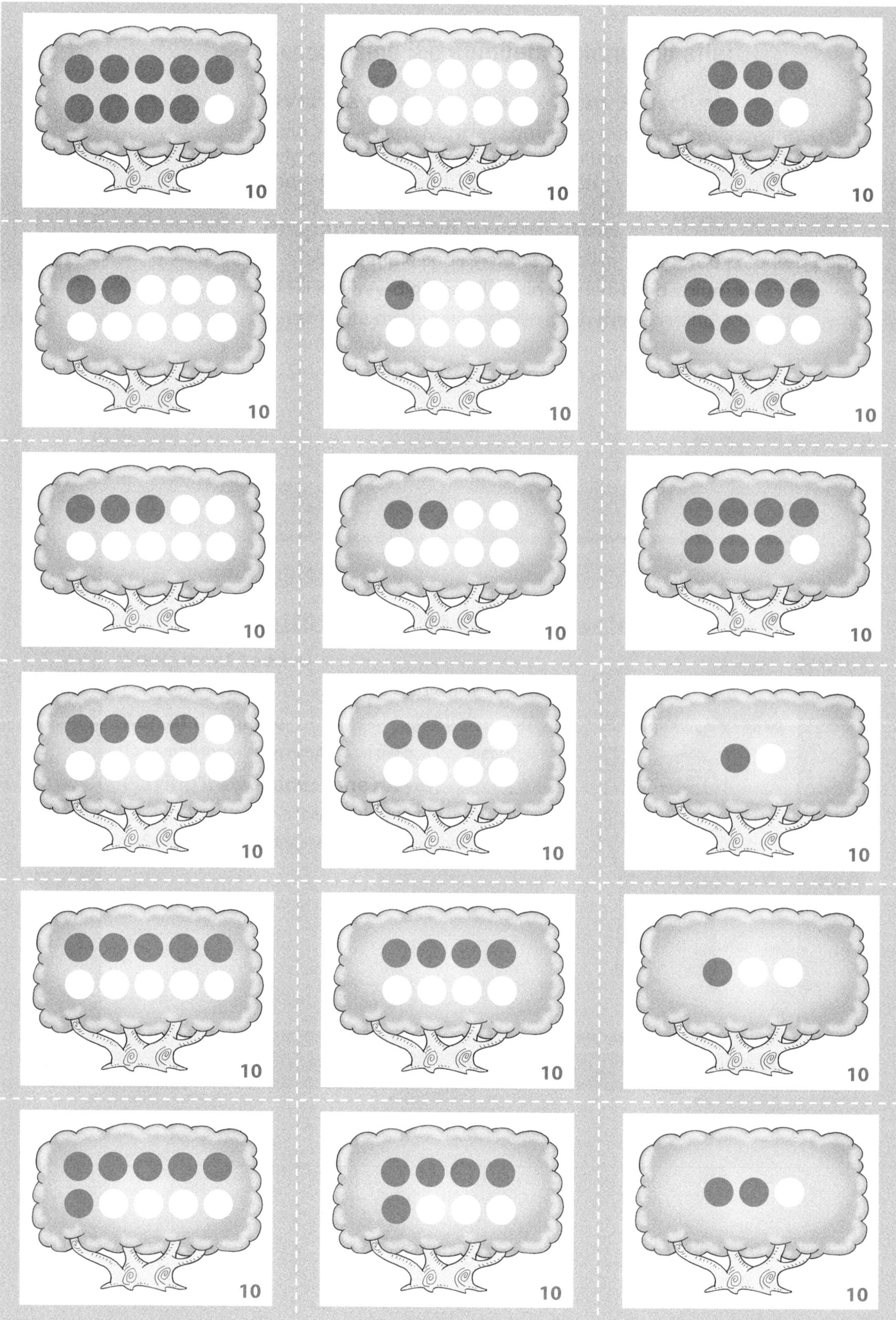

Recognising mixed numbers

Overview: Fraction Rummy, Memory and Snap

Fraction Rummy, Memory and Snap are three games designed to make children more familiar with fraction families.

Preparation and organisation

- Copy the game cards onto coloured paper.
- Laminate and cut out the cards.
- Store in a ziplock bag.

I am learning to recognise fraction families.

Fraction Rummy

Equipment needed
- Game cards

Aim of the game
To be the first to collect three cards that all have the same value.

Playing instructions (up to four players)
- The dealer shuffles all the cards and deals four to each player.
- The dealer places all but one of the remaining cards face down in a pile and puts one "discard card" face up next to the pile.
- The dealer starts and picks up either the discard card or the top card from the pile then discards one card from their hand and puts it face up next to the pile.
- The game continues in a clockwise direction.
- The first player to collect a "family" of fractions is the winner.

11

I am learning to recognise fraction families.

Fraction Memory

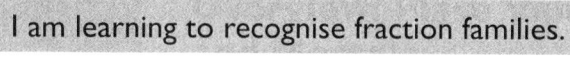

Equipment needed
- Game cards

Aim of the game
To collect as many pairs of cards as possible, where each pair consists of two fraction symbols of the same value.

Playing instructions (two players)
- Spread all of the cards face down over the floor or another large, flat surface.
- In turn each player turns over two cards.
- If the fraction symbols on the two cards have the same value, the player sets them aside as a pair.
- Play until all the cards have been paired up. The player who has collected more pairs is the winner.

11

I am learning to recognise fraction families.

Fraction Snap

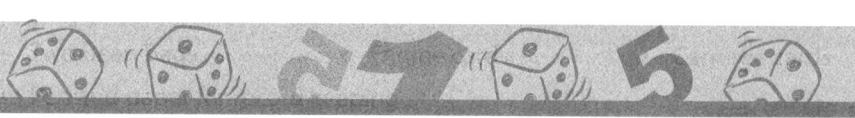

Equipment needed
- Game cards

Aim of the game
To get all of the game cards.

Playing instructions (two players)
- Deal out all the cards equally between the players, who hold them face down in a small pile.
- In turn, each player places their top card face up in the middle.
- If the card they place shows the same value as the card that is immediately underneath it in the middle pile, both of the players race to be first to "snap" the pile. The player who is first gets the pile and puts it at the bottom of their own pile of cards.
- The game continues until one player has all the cards.

11

No Nonsense Number Games Series

These games will keep the fun in maths learning! This series provides high-quality support for numeracy teaching and learning for 5–11 year olds.

The games and activities help develop related number knowledge including number identification, number sequence and order, addition and subtraction, grouping and place value, and number facts. Child-friendly instructions for games, and links between each game and activities in the No Nonsense Number and the Number Counts books are provided.

ISBN 978-1-908736-22-2

PB00143